LIVING AS A PERSON OF DESTINY

A 5-week study on living with
Destiny and sharing God's Love

by Evelyn Burt

Evelyn Burt
Proverbs 3:5-6

DEDICATION

I would first of all like to dedicate this book to the God who gave me the stories in the first place! Without Him, there would be nothing in my life worth sharing! May this book honor Him in every way! All proceeds from this book will be directed to ministry that will help equip and train others to know about this awesome God I serve.

Also, to my Dad who taught me at an early age about this Jesus, who I have grown to love more and more over my lifetime. He taught me and encouraged me to always take advantage of opportunities to share my faith with others. He prayed over me every day of his life, that was a priceless gift! I am humbled by the tremendous prayer that has been invested in me. I know "...to whom much is given, much is required!" Luke 12:48 (AMP)

Finally, I would like to dedicate this book in memory of my late husband, Bob (Rear Admiral Robert F. Burt), who always saw so much more potential in me than I ever saw in myself, and to my daughters, Lisa and Leanne, who have been with me through the good times and the hard times and have always stood by me with their loving support, and to my grandchildren and great-grandchildren that this book will inspire them to continue to grow in their faith and fulfill the destiny God has in mind for them.

TABLE OF CONTENTS

Week 4: Possibilities

Week 5: Peace

Final Thoughts

ACKNOWLEDGMENTS

I want to thank the many people who have listened to me share my stories one on one over the years and encouraged me to write a book. Many of them are people I had never met before. After sharing with them some of my stories, these people believed my experiences would be an encouragement to readers. I have shared my personal life experiences with many people, whether on a plane, in hospital waiting rooms, on cruise ships, shopping, or wherever God provided a "Divine Appointment". When you are looking for opportunities you will discover they are everywhere!

I especially want to thank my Pastor Wes Davis, who asked me to write a book or two! His encouragement and belief in me sparked a determination that helped make this happen. I want to thank Jenni Waldron who gave me a deadline to work by and contributed to the reflection and study questions at the end of each segment. There were many others who offered their editorial skills to make this book a reality: Roz Rude; my sister, Barbra Bynoe; my son-in-law, Jeremy Johnson; friends, Mavis Judkins, Leota Emery and Dr. Dorie Erickson. Thank you to Kylie Danskin, my granddaughter-in-law, who helped with the graphics and cover design. A special thanks to Doug Harkness for the time he invested in preparing this book to go to the printers. I want to thank my family and friends who have stood by me with encouraging words and support. Many prayers have played a significant role in its completion.

To God be all the Glory!

"For I know the plans I have for you, declares the Lord, plans to prosper you and not to harm you, plans to give you hope and a future."

Jeremiah 29:11 (NIV)

WEEK 1
INTRODUCTION

I am so glad you have chosen to read this book. It is my first, and I am excited to share my personal stories with you. I am an ordinary woman who faces many of the same challenges you do. I met Jesus at a young age, and over the years I have learned that God created me with a *"Destiny"* in mind. Throughout this book I will be talking about four specific P's or principles; *Power, Purpose, Possibilities and Peace,* which I believe He wants to equip us with as we walk through life fulfilling His destiny for us. There are many more I could write about, but for this book, these are the ones I will be addressing. It is my prayer as you read through these pages that your heart will be filled with hope and encouragement

I attended a church in San Diego, many years ago, with a banner hanging in the lobby that read: "There are no strangers here, only friends we've never met!" I decided to adopt this phrase as my personal motto.

When I was growing up as a teenager, I would often daydream about my future destiny. It went something like this:

One day I will meet and marry a handsome young man who loves Jesus. We will be active in a local church. We will live on the edge of a forest in a little house with a white picket fence around it. We will raise two children and live happily ever after!

Well, as sweet and simplistic as this may sound, God had other plans for my life. The following is a little peek at how my life has played out as an adult living out my Destiny!

I did meet and marry a handsome, young man named Bob, who loved Jesus. It was while attending Bible College that I met and fell in love with him. We married while he was still attending college and started enjoying our new life together as youth pastors, but that is probably about as close to my teenage dream as it gets!

School was becoming less important to us after we were married. I had my "Mrs." Degree (a younger generation may not identify with this
degree but it simply means I became Mrs. Burt). and we knew my husband would not be able to graduate with his class, since he was coming up short on the number of credits required to do so. Bills were mounting up and we decided working full time would be a better solution to making ends meet, rather than going to school and adding to our debt. We made the decision that Bob would drop out of school a semester before graduation. This was probably not the wisest thing to do, however, we had each other and we all know you can live on love for a long time when you are young! Life has a way of sidetracking us sometimes!

It was a couple of years later that our life would

take another turn. The Vietnam War was winding down, but the military draft was still in effect, and Bob could see his number was coming up. He knew he would soon be drafted into the U.S. Army and he decided that he would prefer to be in the Navy rather than the Army. He immediately went to the local Navy Recruiting Office and joined the enlisted ranks as a sailor.

This was never part of my plan for my life. If anyone would have told me that Bob would one day become a sailor in the Navy, I am certain I would have never married him! I recall that the whole idea of becoming a Navy wife was terrifying to me. This young wife went to her knees in prayer, taking her concerns to God and praying faithfully for her husband to be strong in his faith.

Fast forwarding, he ended up spending 36 years in the Navy. I discovered I thoroughly enjoyed being a Navy wife and the adventures it afforded our family. Seven of those years he was enlisted.

We were blessed with two daughters, who learned to adapt to our military life of moving, on average, every two years. Bob was a faithful, loving husband and a great dad to his "girls". I never once doubted his faithfulness to me. He was a great role model for others to look up to.

Years later, our family grew to include two sons-in-law, five grandchildren and two great-grandchildren. We had a great life together, although it was not always smooth sailing. There were many challenges including deployment separations, robberies, health issues, financial struggles and isolation from family and hometown friends. Each challenge has produced a story of God's provision and grace. Through them we learned to depend on Jesus for everything we needed.

As I reflect on my dreams as a teenager and compare them to the way my life has turned out, I see how God has gone ahead and prepared the way for me to walk toward the destiny He planned for me. He must be, as our Creator, a little amused at all the plans we make for ourselves. He is the one who designed us to be equipped with *His Power, His Purpose, His Possibilities, and His Peace.* When you ask Him to develop the principles of these four P's in your own life, you will discover this is a step towards becoming a *Person of Destiny* and living a satisfying, purpose-filled life!

My life has been filled with far more adventure and excitement than I ever dreamed possible! It has also had its share of pain and sorrow, but the good news is that God has been with me every step of the way! I am believing He will speak to many of you as you read the following pages. May you be encouraged to step out by faith and either continue or begin *Living as a Person of Destiny!* He has a plan for each one of us, and all we have to do is yield to Him and He will take care of the rest.

THE PEA POD STORY

This study is all about learning to "LIVE AS A PERSON OF DESTINY" with the principles of the 4 P's. Each week, we will walk through one of the "Four P's in a P.O.D" (Person of Destiny). I will be sharing personal stories from my own life to illustrate the way God uses ordinary circumstances to equip us with these extraordinary P's.

When I was first writing this study, I thought of the phrase "Four P's in a P.O.D" and God confirmed the concept right away. I even found a paper towel roll shortly afterward that had – you guessed it – 4 peas in a pod.

(This is a photo of the actual paper towel!)

So, I started writing. I knew the concept would be easy to remember, but it was a little ironic. The irony is, I don't even like peas! In fact, I recall growing up we were taught to eat everything set before us whether we liked it or not.

One day we were visiting some distant relatives, and clearly they did not know me very well, because they served peas with the meal. I remember carefully planting four peas on my plate to comply with my dad's rule of eating some of everything and I thought I was doing good. But as the bowl of peas was passed around the table there were little chuckles emerging as one by one family members were taking note of the "four peas" on my plate. Everyone seemed to find humor in it except my dad, who proceeded to put two heaping spoonfuls of peas on my plate. He wanted to make sure I understood that I should have put enough peas on my plate so no one would have noticed or suspected that I didn't like them. Lesson learned and not forgotten!

Of course, what we will be talking about in this book aren't the peas you eat . . . these are a different type of P's and the P.O.D. is a Person of Destiny! I am going to relate each "P" to a principle I believe God equips us with in order to live out the life of destiny He designed for each of us.

The 4 P's are:

1. POWER

2. PURPOSE

3. POSSIBLITIES

4. PEACE

Here is my prayer for you: That through my stories and your time with those with which you are gathering, you will see how God desires to equip you with all four of these "P's" so you can truly live as a Person of Destiny!

- Take a moment and write a prayer to God for each of the four P's. Ask Him for what you hope to experience in each area through this study.

    Power

    Purpose

    Possibilities

    Peace

- Circle the P above that you are most afraid you could never experience. Write to God, below, the reason for feeling that way.

- Read Psalm 139:1-18 – What does this say about God's plan for you? (vs 16) His love for you? (vs 17)

- Read Ephesians 2:10 – What good things do you believe God planned for you long ago?

1. Why did you choose to take part in this study? What do you hope to get out of it?

2. Which "P" are you most interested in learning about and why?

3. What is something this group can pray with you about?

"But you will receive power when the Holy Spirit comes on you; and you will be my witnesses in Jerusalem, and in all Judea and Samaria, and to the ends of the earth."

Acts 1:8 (NIV)

WEEK 2
Discovering Power to be Bold!

I was born in a family poor by material standards, but rich in their knowledge and relationship with Jesus Christ. As I grew up, I was taught about Jesus at home, through Sunday School classes, youth groups and church. My parents had given me a solid foundation in my knowledge of God and of Jesus. However, it takes more than knowledge of God to truly make a difference in your life.

I was quite shy as a young person and would have never dreamed of talking to anyone I didn't know. I would be totally embarrassed if someone I was with would be so bold as to ask a total stranger for something as simple as directions. At twelve years old all that shyness began to quickly fade away.

We were having special services at our church, and I recall the minister sharing verses from the Bible that talked about how everyone is born with a sinful nature. We all have done things that we are not proud of, and he said the Bible calls it sin. He told how God loved us so much that He sent His son Jesus to come to Earth to pay the penalty for our sins by dying on the cross. He went on to say that we could invite Jesus to forgive us of our sins and He would even remove the guilt from our past mistakes. The minister encouraged us to invite the Holy Spirit into our lives so we could receive the "Power" spoken of in Acts 1:8 to become witnesses for Christ.

I remember recognizing my need to get a fresh start with God. That night I made a serious commitment to Jesus and invited him to come into my life, and to fill me with the Holy Spirit so that I, too, would have boldness to talk to others about him. It was a life-changing experience as I took my relationship with Jesus to be more than just knowledge about him. I committed my life to Jesus and asked God to forgive me of the things I had done in my life that had not pleased him. I am sure I had done that many times before, but there was something different this time. Maybe it was the first time I began to understand the importance of taking my relationship seriously. I know that as I invited the Holy Spirit to come into my life, a change began to take place. It was more than just head knowledge about God and His love for me, I was actually experiencing a personal relationship with Jesus Christ, empowered by the Holy Spirit to live out my new life in Christ.

I will never forget that night or the change it made in me. I sensed God's presence coming into my life in a new way. I felt immersed in God's love and excited about my new life. My awareness of God was heightened and I noticed my shyness becoming less and less. I found myself easily talking to others openly about my faith. I would invite my friends to come to church with me. From that point on, I began to develop a "powerful" boldness and desire to talk about my faith and my enthusiasm for God.

Maybe you can relate to the awkwardness that shyness presents at times. The feeling of not fitting into a conversation, or feeling all alone in a crowded room. You are not alone! I want to encourage you to invite God's power into your life, and give you the confidence to overcome those fears. He delights in turning our weaknesses into His strength through the Power of the Holy Spirit.

"For though a righteous man falls seven times, he rises again, but the wicked are brought down by calamity."
Proverbs 24:16 (NIV)

Discovering "Power" to Overcome!

Sometimes we find ourselves facing challenges which are out of the ordinary. I discovered, as we are learning to live out the Destiny God designed for us, there will be obstacles! Satan is on a mission to distract us, run interference, discourage us and anything else he can think of to slow us down and get us off the path God has set out for us. However, with the Holy Spirit residing in us, he is able to equip us with all the "power" we need to overcome any obstacle that comes our way. This next story is about the power I received from God to complete the mission He had orchestrated for me.

I had been invited to be the guest speaker at a ladies luncheon in Newport, Rhode Island, on May 6, 2006. On Tuesday, May 2, Bob and I went out for dinner. Our youngest daughter, Leanne and I were talking on my cell phone as Bob and I walked toward the restaurant. As I went to step up on the sidewalk, I tripped and fell on my hands and knees on the pavement. I was stunned, my cell phone went flying and there I was, on all fours trying to determine how badly I was hurt. The left palm of my hand was stinging with pain and I noticed it was all scuffed up, close to bleeding, but just minor scrapes. I fully expected my knees to be bleeding and have holes in the knees of my pants.

As I slowly pulled myself to my feet, I was surprised, my pants were not torn, no broken skin, just a big goose egg below my right knee. I was confident, my injuries were minor, save the embarrassment of falling! I felt in my spirit, this was a spiritual battle, and I was going to be okay. It was an attempt from the enemy to mess me up and, if possible, spoil my plans of going to Newport to speak. Bob and I were so thankful for God's hand of protection on me. That was Tuesday.

On Thursday night, May 4th, as I was packing and getting ready to leave the next morning for Newport, I experienced another "spiritual attack". I was doing laundry and taking clothes out of the dryer, as I reached down to pick up the laundry basket, my little toe caught the door frame of the laundry closet and I heard a "snap." Even my husband heard the snapping sound and he was in a different room! I was reasonably sure I had either broken or cracked my little toe. It immediately began to swell and turn black and blue. All 1 could think about was what horrible timing! Here I was getting ready to fly to Rhode Island the next morning to speak to the women on Saturday and after my return I had two more trips lined up. I would be traveling with my husband to visit the Naval bases in Hawaii, followed by another week in Okinawa, where I would have the opportunity to meet with and encourage the chaplain spouses whose husbands were stationed there. I was envisioning myself trying to get around with a broken/fractured toe over the next two weeks. I couldn't even bear the thought of putting on a closed-toe shoe for my speaking engagement.

As these thoughts were swirling through my head, all at once my thoughts were quieted with the sense that this was, again, an attack from the enemy to keep me from going to Newport. Bob said "I think I'd better call Maryanne, and tell her you will not be able to come." I suddenly sensed "a warrior-like mentality" rising up within me and quickly replied, "No I am going! This is an attack from the enemy and I will not let him get the victory." I believed God had given me a message for those women, and the Devil was doing everything he could to stop me. I was going!

I didn't get much sleep that night. The next morning my foot continued to be swollen and very black and blue. At this point, I was excited about what was going on. I felt so strongly that God must have something special in store for all of us at the retreat.

One of the Chaplain's wives met me at the airport. It was my first time meeting her and we felt an instant "kindred spirit" between us. She picked me up at Providence, RI and we drove back to Newport. It was a beautiful sunny day and we enjoyed going to lunch and shopping around in the quaint downtown waterfront area on the cobblestone streets. I was amazed, I had no difficulty with my walking in spite of the bruised and injured toe. I spent the night in the home of my friend, Maryanne, who had invited me to come and speak. I shared with her the events of my week and the confidence I had that God must have something special for all of us since it seemed as if the Devil was doing all he could to prevent me from being there.

Saturday morning we were walking out the door

to go to the luncheon. Maryanne and her husband were pointing out the landscaping they were having done at their place. As I was looking around and admiring it all, I walked right off their deck and fell flat on my chest! I couldn't believe it. What was happening to me? It was the worst fall I have ever taken as an adult. The pain was intense and I wasn't sure if I would be able to get up from the fall. As I lay on the pavement, I was in pain and crying. I had new glasses on, and now they were totally bent out of shape. One arm was going straight up and the other stretched out to the side. Fortunately, the lenses were not scratched.

I recall asking my friend, who was a nurse, "Maryanne, what is happening to me? Do you think I am okay?" She responded she wasn't sure! I told her, "I am not usually so clumsy as I have been this week and am concerned that something may be really wrong with me." Once again, I heard in my spirit, "You are going to be okay, this is a spiritual attack!" It was another final attempt to keep me from speaking to the women. I was quite shaken up, and Maryanne's husband, Bert, helped me to my feet. We went back in the house and I took inventory of the damage.

Once again, I could not believe I did not have holes in my pant legs or my suit jacket. I was a bit dirty, but nothing that couldn't be brushed off. My left hand was, again, all scuffed up and this time I scraped my knuckles to the point of bleeding on my right hand. Bert managed to straighten my glasses out so I could wear them. All in all, I had this overwhelming confidence I was going to be okay! I think the stress of it all got the best of me for a little bit and I found tears to be a helpful release. Within half an hour we were once again on our way, with a determination to be used by God and be a blessing to these women.

When we arrived, the luncheon began. I found it difficult to even hold a paper plate in my left hand, the pain was so intense. I was certain I had either fractured or broken my wrist. Maryanne asked me how I was doing and I told her I was in a lot of pain and expressed my concerns of a possible fracture or broken wrist. She told me she would be taking me to the E.R. for X-rays once our event was over.

I was introduced to the ladies and was carefully holding my wrist as I walked up to the front of the room. As I began to share with them the events of the week leading up to that morning, I suddenly realized I was talking with both of my hands. I began shaking my left hand in disbelief! There was absolutely no pain! I excitedly shared with the women that I had at that precise moment, received a supernatural, instantaneous healing! My hand was completely normal, no pain at all. Maryanne kept motioning me not to move it, but I repeatedly waved it back and forth declaring there was absolutely no pain! I was experiencing a miraculous healing and all of these ladies were witnessing it.

By this point I had all of their attention and I was ready to begin with my stories I had prepared to share with them. God had won the victory throughout this spiritual battle. How I praise God for the Holy Spirit that kept assuring me that I was going to be okay, that I was simply dealing with spiritual warfare! What I had experienced was the Power of God at work on my behalf, equipping me to carry out the plan He had for me!

I share this story with you to remind you that sometimes it's not just about the events that seem to be happening to us, but it is the opportunities God uses from these events to point us to His power to overcome and give us an incredible testimony to share with others.

Can you think of a time when you were excited about doing something you believed God had prompted you to do? You may have shared your thoughts with someone who did not share your same enthusiasm for the idea and you became discouraged. Or you may have actually attempted to do what God asked you to do and you felt like your efforts were a total disaster! Perhaps the more you thought about the idea, you questioned whether or not you had heard anything from God at all.

I believe these are all very natural reactions that we can experience when we begin to step outside of our comfort zone. The Devil, the Enemy, is on a mission to thwart God's work. He uses discouragement and the feelings of inadequacy to keep you distracted from how God wants to use your life to give Him Glory. Satan has proven to be very effective at times. Our job is to be mindful of his strategy and look instead to God for our confidence.

We need to ask God to give us that "warrior-like mentality" that will press us on to complete the task, no matter the obstacles that come our way. Remember, God wants to lead us, and He knows the enemy's tactics and how to overcome them! We can trust God to help us persevere and come out stronger than ever as we do what He has asked us to do. Others will be blessed, and we be will, too! You never know—there could be a "powerful" miracle waiting for you on the other side of your "obstacle course".

- Read Acts 1:8. What does this say about God and His Power? What does this say about you?

- Read 1 John 4:4. What does it mean that the Spirit that is in you is greater than the Spirit who lives in the world?

- Is there somewhere in your life that you need to experience God's power? Where?

- When was the last time you heard from God? What did He say to you?

- Finish this sentence: If I were not afraid, I would . . .

- Write down the names of 5 people you know who need to experience the life-giving power of Jesus

1. When did you first say yes to Jesus? Have you?

2. What is the difference between God's Power and your strength?

3. How do you finish the sentence: If I were not afraid, I would . . .

4. What is something this group can pray with you about?

"I will praise the Lord, who
counsels me; even at night
my heart instructs me."
Psalm 16:7 (NIV)

purpose

WEEK 3
Discovering God's PURPOSE
Through a Dream

In my journey as a Christian, I had received the *"power"* to be the "Person Of Destiny" God created me to be. It was not a problem for me to talk about my faith. I was about to discover there was more to living out my Christian faith than just talking about it. As a committed Christian, I needed to share on *"purpose"* the Good News of Jesus with others!

This experience happened when I was 20 years old. I was a new bride and worked as a clerk typist in a wood testing laboratory. There was only one other woman who worked with me. All the rest were great family men. I knew a couple of them were Christians and they all knew I went to church and was active in my faith, but I had never personally talked to anyone about their faith in God. It was easy for me to talk about what God was doing in my life, but I never pursued anyone to see if they understood their need for God.

One night I had a dream I truly believe was inspired by God, Himself. In my dream, it was the end of time. There was a long line of people waiting to have God accept them into heaven. One of my co-workers was standing in line in front of me. His name was Jim and he was probably in his early- to mid-30's – nice guy, good family man, great worker. I recall him standing patiently with his hands clasped in front of him, waiting his turn. When his turn came, God looked at him and said "Depart from me, I never knew you, you worker of iniquity". (Those words are actually from a verse in the Bible, Matthew 7:23 in the Old King James Version. Now, "iniquity" is not a common word we use in our everyday language, but it refers to sin.)

By the world's standards there was really nothing wrong with Jim. The problem is that God does not look at us through the eyes of the world! He looks at us through His eyes of Holiness. If he doesn't see Jesus in our life, then He does not know us. There was a look of shock on Jim's face as he turned to see who God was speaking to. God looked straight at Jim and repeated the same words again, "Depart from me, I never knew you, you worker of iniquity". Now Jim was horrified! He couldn't believe that God was actually rejecting him. What had he done wrong? He was a good person, lived a great life, surely there must be some mistake!

I was in line behind Jim and when I stood before God, He looked at me and said, "Enter in, thou good and faithful servant, I am well pleased!" (Another verse from the Bible in Matthew 25:23.) This doesn't mean I had lived a perfect life. What it does mean is I had invited Christ into my life and was living my life on *"purpose"* for Him. The next scene I will never forget, nor do I ever want to forget as long as I live. Jim looked at me and said, "Evelyn, you mean to tell me you knew how to make sure you were going to spend eternity in heaven and you never cared enough to tell me? I thought you were my friend!" The look Jim gave me in my dream has been etched in my mind ever since. I woke up immediately and was so thankful it was only a dream!

The next morning when I got to work, I found Jim and told him I needed to talk to him. I had something important to share. We sat down at a table and I began to relay the dream I had about him the night before. God immediately gave me the words to follow up the dream by telling him that all of us need Jesus in our lives. We all come into this world in a state of sin. We have all made mistakes and have regrets in our lives. The Bible calls these things "sin" ("For all have sinned and fall short of the glory of God." Romans 3:23 NIV). God had a plan to remedy the sin in our lives by sending His only son, Jesus, born of a virgin, into the world to live a perfect, holy, life and become a sacrifice for our sins. Jesus, who had never done a single thing wrong or committed any sin, died a criminal's death on a cross for our sins. It is only when we acknowledge by faith that Jesus is truly the son of God and invite him to take away all our past sins and remove the guilt, that we are truly set free to live our lives for him, and are assured of eternal life in heaven when we die. The most meaningful and exciting part of Jesus dying on the cross for us is this: not only did he take the penalty for our sins, but three days later he rose from the dead, promising all who believe in him and accept his sacrifice for their sins will have eternal life in heaven.

I continued to share with Jim his need to invite Christ into his life so that he, too, could know without a doubt that he would spend eternity in heaven. I asked him if he would like to do that right then? He looked at me and smiled, patted me on the shoulder and said, "I think this is sweet of you to share this with me. I think it is great for you to believe, but it is just not for me."

With that I looked at him and said, " Jim, I am certain there will be people that look at me the way you did in my dream last night, but you will not be one of them. I really care about you and as often as the Lord brings you to my mind I will be praying that you will see your need for Jesus in your life."

That ended our conversation that day and there were no hard feelings. I just prayed for Jim, that one day he would know God's love and forgiveness, and invite Jesus into his life, and have the assurance that he would spend eternity in heaven.

It was not long afterwards that my husband joined the Navy as an enlisted man and we moved out of the area. Throughout the years, the Lord would periodically remind me to pray for Jim, and I would.

Seven years later, Bob got out of the Navy in order to complete college and seminary in preparation to become a Chaplain in the Navy. We moved back to his hometown in Oregon where we had lived. During that time we were attending a large Christian Conference in Eugene, Oregon. To my surprise, during one of the breaks, I ran into my old co-worker, Jim, from years ago.

I couldn't believe he was there! I asked him if this meant he was a Christian now? He said "yes"! I was so excited to see him and I reminded him of the dream I had shared with him years ago and asked if he had remembered it. He said "No."

Later that day I was talking to his wife. She told me how he was a new Christian, and to please keep praying for him. I ran into Jim a little later during the conference and he said, "Oh, by the way, I didn't really forget that dream." I was certain that he hadn't because it had such a powerful impact on me personally, that I had to believe it was a "God dream". That dream has continued to fuel my *"Purpose"* for not only sharing my faith, but giving others an opportunity to respond.

Maybe you haven't had a dream like mine, or maybe you have. There may have been times as a Christian, where you have sensed God speaking to you, or prompting you to share your faith with another person. You may have immediately sensed an uneasiness and nervousness about doing so. If you have had concerns of offending them, or not knowing exactly what to say, you are not alone! It can seem kind of scary the first time you talk to someone about the Lord. But don't let that stop you. Have you ever thought that maybe this was the *"Purpose"* God had in mind when He brought that person into your life?

I want to encourage you to ask God to give you ears to hear Him speak, and to give you a willing heart to share His love with others.   The more you share, the less you will be intimidated by fear.

"The thief comes only to steal and kill and destroy; I have come that they may have life, and have it to the full."
John 10:10 (NIV)

Discovering God's Purpose in a Heart Attack

Sometimes we have experiences and we try to figure out why an event happened the way it did. Do you know what I am talking about? I had one of those experiences when we were living in the Memphis, Tennessee area.

My husband and I had been invited to attend a church in the community with friends we had made. At this particular church, it was common practice to open up the altars for those who would like to pray when the service concluded. I always liked that because I grew up with that kind of worship service. Sometimes I would go down and pray but not necessarily after every service. Little did I know that this Sunday would be no ordinary Sunday.

The service had concluded, the invitation to pray was made and Bob and I began to visit with some of the people sitting behind us. My husband suggested we go to the foyer to visit. Just as we were heading for the foyer I suddenly had an urgent burden to pray. My heart began pounding and I recognized the feeling—someone needed my prayers and they needed them right now. I excused myself and told Bob that I needed to go pray for a few minutes. He said, "Fine, we will be in the foyer."

By the time I got to the altar, I was sobbing with this burden. I recall being on my knees, asking God to intervene in whatever way He needed for the situation. I did not know who needed these prayers, but I felt strongly that the need was urgent. After a few minutes of praying intensely for the need, the burden lifted. I was about to get up and leave when suddenly, instead of a burden to pray, I now had a strange new feeling in my chest. There was such a heaviness, a pain that I felt from the front of my chest clear through to my back. I remember praying, "Oh God, what is this pain, I don't know it, is it spiritual pain or physical pain?"

About that time I felt a hand on my shoulder and a lady asked me if I was having chest pain, and if I did, maybe I needed to go to the emergency room. My response was, "I am just praying." She was someone who would pray with people at the altars and she heard me ask God about my pain. Then she immediately prayed, "Dear God, we ask for your wisdom in this situation right now, in the Name of Jesus." The moment she finished that sentence I felt every ounce of strength leave my body. I was already on my knees but my entire body slumped to the floor like a pile of humanity. I had no strength. I recall hearing her tell someone to "Get me an aspirin." By this time I was a little embarrassed and thought, *I am just going to get up.* I started to get up and began to pass out. As I lay on the floor, the pastor came over and laid his hand on my chest and began to earnestly pray that God would take control of my heart, in the name of Jesus! The next thing I knew someone had called an ambulance, I had been given an aspirin and I was being hoisted onto a gurney headed for the hospital.

In the meantime, someone went out to the foyer

and told my husband they thought his wife was having medical problems at the altar.

Once in the ambulance, the medic immediately squirted a shot of nitroglycerin under my tongue and asked me what level of pain I was experiencing. I told him it was "four or five." We were probably halfway to the hospital when he asked me if I still had that chest pain. I said "Yes." He radioed into the hospital and told them I was not responding to the nitroglycerin. They told him to give me another dose. By the time we got to the hospital the pain was totally gone, I was completely embarrassed by all the commotion and I was ready to get out of there and go have some lunch. But it wasn't going to happen all that fast.

I had been checked into the emergency room and plans were made to run some tests on me in about an hour to determine what had caused the concern. About 45 minutes had passed and Bob and our friend, Lowell, who had invited us to church, were standing there talking when I suddenly had another episode just like I had earlier at church.

I was immediately whisked up into another room where they did a heart catheterization on me. I could see my heart on the monitor and I heard the nurse say two times: "Look at this woman's heart! This is a miracle, this is a miracle!" It was obvious that I had suffered a mild heart attack, but there was absolutely no blockage of the arteries and no apparent reason for the heart attack. My heart was a picture of good health except that it showed I had suffered a mild heart attack. It was at that moment I realized my sudden burden to pray at church was actually for myself. It was me that was standing in need of immediate prayer.

I truly believe God intervened that day and spared my life. We have quite a history of heart problems in my family. My mom died of congestive heart failure when I was 16 and she was only 40. My dad also dealt with heart problems, having had two quintuple bypass surgeries in his life. High blood pressure is not an uncommon issue in my family history. I was kept in the hospital for five days while they continued to try and solve the mystery of my heart attack. I kept telling them I was a miracle — God had intervened and spared my life! They never did come up with an exact cause for the heart attack. But what they did discover was I have a blood disorder called Leiden Factor V. This simply means my blood tends to clot. The doctors suspect that I did have a blood clot but by the time they were able to do the heart catheterization the clot had moved on and broken up.

I went home from the hospital feeling just fine. I decided that maybe having a heart attack wasn't so bad after all. But I knew that wasn't true — it could have been fatal! It was a mystery to me as to why I had that experience. What was it all about anyway? I almost felt guilty as people would ask me for months afterwards how I was feeling. I received more cards and letters from people I didn't even know than I had ever received in my life. As I thought about it, my husband was pretty shaken by the whole experience and he had put the word out to every Chaplain in the U.S Navy to please pray for his wife.

Should it have been a surprise that this didn't seem like such a big deal to me? I had received more prayer for the three months following my heart attack than I had ever received before. God is so good and prayer is very powerful! I did not have to go through the surgery that most heart attack victims undergo, but I do believe God touched me and may have even spared my life. I cannot answer why some people are spared and some are not. As I questioned God about the meaning behind all of this, I sensed Him speaking to my heart. This involved two things: 1) it was a test, and 2) it was a spiritual battle. The test was one of obedience. What if I had not followed my heart's prompting to immediately go pray when I was at the church? Would I be here today telling you this story or would my life have ended that Sunday morning? I don't know the answer, I am just thankful I didn't hesitate to go and pray. The other thing I felt God speak to my heart was this: the enemy of our soul will go to great lengths to destroy God's work.

I have a heart for evangelism and God has used me many times to share His love with other people. Satan does not like that, and when we are out doing what God has called us to do, we become a threat to his work. If the Devil could have snuffed my life out that day, I would be one less Christian he would have to deal with. But I thank God that He goes before me and fights my battles. I am on the winning team and no matter what the enemy tries to do to stop me, God can turn the situation around and use it for His glory and purposes.

I cannot tell you how many opportunities I have had to share this story with others. As a result of discovering I have Leiden Factor V blood, I was told I would be a Coumadin patient the rest of my life. The first year following my heart attack I had to go in almost every week to have my blood tested. Sometimes it seemed to be such a time waster. But then I began to take advantage of opportunities to listen to other patients tell their stories. Many times God gave me the opportunity and the words to share and encourage their hearts in their faith. Sometimes I had the privilege of praying with patients, and in some instances even with staff, for the needs they were sharing with me. I took Coumadin for 13 years and was told at my last exam that there was no longer any evidence of my heart attack or a need to take Coumadin. I believe God completely healed me!

It is my prayer that this story has touched your heart and encouraged you to think about what God has done in your life, and the stories He has given you to share on *"purpose"* with others. Please be encouraged to thank God for the trials He sees you through here on earth. Know that He desires to use these times of testing to strengthen your faith in Him, and prepare you to bring glory to Him and encouragement to others. My heart attack gave me another *"purpose"*, or opportunity, to impact lives for Jesus!

- Read Matthew 28:19. Who is Jesus talking to in this verse? What does that mean for you?

- We all have a purpose to share the saving power of Jesus with those we meet. But, we also have other things that give us purpose. God has given each of us gifts to share. Take some time to pray and write out in one paragraph what you believe your purpose is. *(It's okay if you don't have anything yet . . .)*

- What would change in your life if you lived ON PURPOSE?

- What is something you have felt God asking you to do that you have chosen not to obey? Take some time to confess to God and ask Him to lead you in your purpose.

- Write a message to your younger self about purpose, sharing the rest of this sentence: I wish I had known when I was your age . . .

1. Have you ever had an experience like Evelyn's in which you shared Jesus with someone? How did it go? What did you do afterwards?

2. Whose responsibility is it to cause others to believe? What's your part? What's God's part?

3. What is something this group can pray with you about?

"In his heart a man plans his course, but
the Lord determines
his steps."
Proverbs 16:9 (NIV)

possibilites

WEEK 4
Discovering Possibilities in the Air!

I would like to tell how God created the *"Possibility"* for me to share His love, forgiveness and eternal life with someone I had never met, nor would have had the opportunity to meet without God creating the *"Possibility"*. God will go to great lengths to make our relationship with Him a reality.

I was flying across the country to Boston and had to change planes in Phoenix, Arizona. As I boarded the plane, I noticed coach went to the left as well as to the right. Typically, you walk to the right through first class and then beyond that, you are in coach. I must have looked a little confused as to which way I should be going when the flight attendant asked to see my ticket. She said, "Oh, follow me, I have a better seat for you than that one. She took me to the other side of the plane. It was the kind that has five seats in the center row and three seats on either side. I followed her as she took me about halfway down the far aisle and asked a gentleman sitting in the aisle seat if he would please let me in to take the window seat. He got up and let me in.

That has never happened to me before, but it did happen that day! So, being the outgoing person I had become, I introduced myself to this gentleman named "Al". I said, "Since we are going to be sitting next to each other for several hours, we'd might as well get acquainted." He quickly let me know he would probably be moving up to first class in a few moments. Then he said, "You don't recognize me do you?" Now I'm thinking I am in trouble. I am probably sitting by some celebrity most people would probably know or recognize, but not me! Then he asked if I had ever heard of the Boston Red Sox? I must admit, I have never been much of a sports enthusiast. I didn't even like recess as a young person in school, unless I could be sitting out in the field with a friend, visiting and making daisy chain necklaces. My husband, on the other hand was quite the sports fan, so I did have some exposure, but not much!

I hesitantly responded, "It's baseball, right?" Then he began listing off a lot of names of celebrities he had personally met, and I am sure would be well known by the average person. However, I am not in that average! I did hear a couple of names I recognized, like John Wayne and Bob Hope! Some of you reading this are probably young enough that those names may not be all that familiar to you.

Suddenly after listening to him I felt inspired to

tell him that I knew someone pretty important too! He looked down at me in surprise and said, "Really?"

I replied, "Yes! Do you want to know who I know?" He said "Sure!" I answered, "His name is Jesus, and he is my best friend! Do you know him?" I asked. Al shook his head, "No". "Do you know anything about his Father, God?" Again, he shook his head, "No", and I asked him if I could tell him about my best friend Jesus, and he responded, "Sure".

Once again, God created a "Possibility" for me to share God's beautiful plan of bringing a right relationship between them and Himself. God gave me the words to clearly and simply share with him how easy it was to ask Jesus to forgive him of his sins and to begin to experience the genuine peace that comes into our lives and gives us the God-confidence that we are in good standing with our Creator.

I asked Al if he would like to invite Jesus into his life and to begin to live for God. He said yes! I told him how I knew God had specifically allowed our paths to cross in order that he might hear about Jesus. After all, he thought he was going to be moving to first class and I was sitting in a seat that I was not assigned to, but rather directed to. This is what I call a "Divine Appointment"! Al bowed his head and began to pray and invite Jesus into his life right there on the airplane! What a blessing to see God at work!

Friends, this is just another example of how much God seeks us out and plants people in our path that are willing to share His love with us.

The stories I have shared with you so far have all dealt with God giving us the *"Power"* to be bold and the *"Purpose"* to reach out of our comfort zone and take advantage of the *"Possibilities"* He creates for us to share His great love with others.

When we begin to ask God for opportunities or *possibilities* to encourage others or share our stories with them, God will provide a listening ear. It is not our job to make someone want to accept Jesus. Our job is to simply share the "good news of the Gospel," and give others an invitation to become part of God's family.

I have found that when I sincerely ask God to give me an opportunity to share His love, He has never failed to bring someone across my path who was eager to listen. It doesn't mean they have all accepted Jesus. It simply means I have planted a "seed" in their lives. Sometimes I plant a seed (the gospel message) and other times I simply water the "seed" others have planted, by sharing stories to cause them to think about the importance of having Jesus in their life. Sometimes, as in this story, I have the blessing to witness and be a part of someone inviting Jesus to come into their life. A chance to give them a brand new start and a new purpose for living! It is truly an exciting and rewarding experience. If you've never done this, I want to encourage you to give it a try with God's help. It is so rewarding!

"Jesus replied, "What is impossible with men is possible with God."
Luke 18:27 (NIV)

Discovering More Possibilities:
Meeting Patsy!

I met Patsy in 2000 while working at a Thomas Kinkade Art Gallery in Memphis, TN. She and her husband were in the area on business and just happened to stop in the gallery to check it out. I soon realized they both loved Jesus, and we were all part of God's great big family. After I learned they would be in the area for a few days, I invited them over to our home for dinner. Now, that was not an ordinary thing for me to do. They agreed to come and we all enjoyed a great evening of fellowship and getting acquainted. We have kept in touch over the years via phone.

Several years had passed since we met these new friends. We were stationed in the Washington, DC area, and they were again on a business trip in that area. They called to see about the *"possibility"* of getting together. We invited them over for dinner and enjoyed another great evening. We both laughed when we asked if we thought we would have even recognized each other if we were to have passed on the street — both of us agreed we had forgotten what each other looked like! I am telling you there are no strangers, only friends we've yet to meet!

A couple more years passed and we still stayed in touch by phone. My husband had retired and we were now living in our retirement home in Silverdale, Washington. Patsy contacted me and invited me to come speak at a Christian Women's Club she was involved with in Michigan. She was also heading up a large community military appreciation event, in which she invited my husband to come speak during the same week. We both went out together and spoke to the groups. It was a wonderful experience for both of us. Getting to know Rob and Patsy and staying in their home for a few days was a wonderful blessing and a treat for us. Sometimes God will surprise us with great experiences simply by taking advantage of the *"possibilities"* He puts in our path!

What if…?

Let's take a closer look at this situation. What if I had not engaged in conversation with them when they came into the gallery? One, I would have been slacking on the job; and two, I would have missed out on meeting a great Christian couple. What if I hadn't been willing to step out of my comfort zone and invite them over for dinner to get better acquainted? We would have missed out on making new friends and we would have missed the opportunity to travel and speak in Michigan. Nor would I have had the experience of seeing the look on my husband's face when I told him we were having company for dinner — people he had never met. Priceless! Now, did I have any idea where my initial conversation with them would have taken me? Not at all, but I am so glad I reached out to them and they responded. It is what I call a Divine Appointment!

"There is none righteous, not one!"

Romans 3:10 (NIV)

Discovering More Possibilities:
My Brother-in-Law John!

Overall, I would say that I get along with most people. But everyone in life will usually find at least one person they find challenging to get along with, let alone love or like! I am no exception. Can you identify with me on that statement?

In my life, it happened to be my husband's brother, my brother-in-law John. Now John was about as opposite as you could get from my husband. He seemed to be born to cause trouble and grief. At least that is how I viewed him. From his early teen years he had been in trouble with the law. He was not a stranger to Juvenile Correctional Centers and as he grew older he spent time in and out of jail; he indulged in drugs and alcohol, and it is safe to say he probably never worked more than 6 months in his entire life. I remember praying that if he was NEVER going to give his life to Christ, that God would be doing us all a favor to take him off planet earth! Now that sounds a bit harsh — and it was! He was a person that was given so many opportunities to change his ways, and yet it didn't seem like he would ever change.

We prayed for years that John would find the Lord and experience the life-changing power of Jesus Christ — that he would have purpose in his life and become a blessing to others. I recall talking to God about John one time and asking the Lord why he was still here — after all it was pretty obvious to me that the man was never going to change.

I distinctly recall the Lord speaking this to my heart: **"You may have given up on John, but I have not"**.

Those words spoke loud and clear to my spirit. He went on to say, **"And just so you know, I love him as much as I love you!"** Ouch! Those words stung! I felt ashamed of my attitude towards him and I asked the Lord to help me see John through His eyes, because when I looked at him through my eyes, I could see no value.

Not long after that prayer, I had a dream about John. Yes, it was a dream, but I truly believe it was a God-inspired dream in answer to my prayers. In my dream, I was sitting at the kitchen table across from John. My husband was on one side of me and my mother in-law was on the other side. I remember seeing John as a totally different person than I had ever known. He was glowing with the love of the Lord; you could see it on his countenance. He began to say how grateful he was to God for what He had done in his life. He went on to say that he knew it was only by God's grace that he was even still alive. It was amazing to me to see the difference I saw in John. He was pleasant to be around and made me feel proud that he was my brother-in-law. This was my dream! That was not reality at that point. I was so encouraged by the dream that it caused me to pray more diligently for John. I began to thank God for his salvation in advance. Well, it wasn't long, and John would do the same kinds of things he had always done, and I would become discouraged and begin to lose sight of the dream God had given me. I was tempted to think that he would never come to know the Lord. I even told God, if He could save John, He could save anyone. Now, it's not that I doubted that God could save John, but I strongly doubted that John would ever surrender to God.

Over the years God gave me three different dreams about John. Each came when I could not see any *"possibility"* of change. I was really discouraged and tempted to give up hope. It was during the times that I failed to see John through God's eyes and I began to see him through my own — and I didn't like what I saw. Following each of those dreams I would pray more diligently and again begin to thank God in advance for John's salvation. I would write letters to John encouraging him to give the Lord an opportunity to work in his life. The Lord opened up my heart toward John, and I began to ask others to join in prayer with me for his salvation. I began to feel a love and compassion for him that I had never known before.

In the summer of 2007, John had been taking illegal drugs and chose to drive his truck. He ended up rolling his truck over an embankment, and it took 90 minutes for paramedics to cut him out of his truck. He was air-lifted to the hospital. No one expected John to live. After being in the hospital for about 3 weeks on life support and an induced coma (the doctors kept him heavily sedated and strapped down — he would become quite violent as his body was going through the withdrawal from the drugs), the doctors called the family in to make a decision as to whether or not he should come off life support. The decision was made that John would not want to continue living in this state and he was taken off life support.

Our prayers were strong, even though we could not communicate with John, we knew God was still able to speak to his spirit — his life still had opportunity to be transformed by God. He was in this coma for about four weeks, and after being taken off life support he began to show signs of life returning! The doctors said his heart was worn out from all the abuse he had inflicted on his body through drugs and alcohol. His heart was only operating at about 20% with little hope of full recovery. For John it was just a matter of time.

But God is so patient. He sent someone to visit John who had lived a good portion of his life the same way John always had, only he had given his life to Christ a few years earlier. When he was visiting John, he began to talk to him about the Lord. John got out of his bed and got down on the floor on his knees and asked his friend to pray with him — he was finally ready to give his life to the Lord!

When I learned that John had given his life to Christ, I wanted to believe and truly be excited, but I struggled with doubt in my own mind. I felt like a doubting Thomas! I wanted to see the change in his life personally. I had that opportunity a couple months later. Although there didn't seem to be a lot of outward change, I could tell from the time I saw him that God had begun a work in his life. He didn't have that hard look about him. Instead, I saw tenderness. I remember talking to John and asking him about his experience with God. I told him I had heard that he had given his life to Christ and asked if he would be willing to tell me about it. He didn't hesitate. He said, "I know I died! And I know I saw God! Bobby (my husband) was there, too!" He continued, "Bobby said, 'John, reach out and take Jesus' hand, He is waiting for you.'" And John did! I cannot tell you the joy that filled my heart as I heard these words come from John's lips and his heart! It was true! God had done the impossible, again!

It was the best weekend I had ever experienced with my brother-in-law. He hung out with us everywhere we went, and he was actually very talkative and fun to be around. The change in his behavior was apparent to me, and I genuinely became excited about this miracle that was taking place in John's life.

Within four months of John giving his life to Christ, he went home to be with the Lord. At his funeral, there were many testimonies of how John's life had changed, from old and young alike. It was a powerful service. He was a baby Christian, but he had made an impact for the Lord on many people's lives. In fact, one man was doing time in jail on a work release program and had been given permission to attend the funeral. He was emotionally moved and tears were flowing down his cheeks. I walked over to him and let him know that God loved him very much. I asked him if he would like to invite Christ into his life. He immediately responded with "I already have!" I asked him to tell me about it. He said after John gave his life to the Lord, John began telling him what God had done for him, and he decided then that he needed Christ to come into his life, too!

That was powerful to me. John was a man who was only a babe in Christ, and by outward appearances did not seem to have much value. He was excited about what God had done in his life and was eager to tell someone else! The person he had shared his new faith with was someone who was ready to respond to God's love. God used John's testimony to create "possibility" for others to have faith in a God who had the power to transform a life. God had turned the impossible into a "possibility!" We had the words "Saved by Grace" inscribed on John's grave marker. I believe those who read these words and who knew what John was in his past, will have hope that there is "possibility" for them, too.

Is there someone in your life you find difficult to like, or love? Have you been praying for them? It can be hard to pray for those you don't particularly care for. What if you asked God to help you see them through His eyes and to give you a supernatural love and compassion for them? I believe it would change the way you pray for them. It can be discouraging at times, but we must keep on believing for the impossible. God truly does specialize in the things we think are impossible. Why not pause, and take a moment to pray for that person now?

Read Matthew 19:26.

- It's important to look back and remember what God has done in our lives. What is a time you have seen God show up in your life? Divine Appointment? Providing in a hard time? Maybe even a miracle?

- Write a list of situations that could have been possibilities that GOD set up (maybe you previously thought they were coincidences or nothing special).

- Is there someone you have given up on that

God has not? How can you pray for that person to experience God?

group discussion

1. What is your favorite place you have traveled?

2. Share a time God set up a possibility for you to live with purpose.

3. If you're comfortable, share the thing you have thought is impossible, but you are committing to believe is possible with God.

4. What is something this group can pray with you about?

"Peace I leave with you; my peace I give you. I do not give to you as the world gives. Do not let your hearts be troubled and do not be afraid".
John 14:27 (NIV)

WEEK 5
Discover Peace in the Midst of Fear

In the military we have what we call "Dream Sheets." It is where you write down your top three choices of duty stations. A detailer (one who assigns military members to their next duty station) will look at it and see if there is an opening for you to go there. Some joke that you will only be assigned there "in your dreams!"

I recall a time when the detailer was discussing our next set of orders. He had told my husband there were three spots that had openings for his position. Two of them were in Okinawa (warm and sunny climate, pretty much year-round) and the other was in Great Lakes, near Chicago, Illinois (typically bitter cold and windy in the winter and hot and humid in the summer). My husband did what he usually does when talking about future orders with his detailer, and said, "Wherever you think would be best, will be fine with us." He asked him to pray about it and let us know. We would consider his choice to be God's will — after all, we do believe God is the ultimate "Detailer" of our lives. I remember offering up a little prayer to God and asking him not to forget that I hate being cold! I had never heard anything about the Chicago area that appealed to me. It sounded bitter, cold. I really did not want to go there at all. Besides that, there were two openings in Okinawa, two out of three chances to go somewhere warm, sounded good to me. In my mind, it was a done deal — no doubt, we would be going to Okinawa.

A week later, my husband called me from work and said he had received his orders. I asked, "Okinawa?" He responded, "No, Great Lakes!" "You've got to be kidding!" was my response. I remember looking up and asking, "God, did you forget that I hate to be cold?" Not only were we going to Great Lakes, but it was January, and we were currently living in Camp Pendleton, just north of San Diego. Chicago had just experienced the worst snowstorm in over thirty years!

The next morning, I was walking in our neighborhood with one of my neighbors, enjoying the balmy breezes, sunshine, palm trees and being in shorts! I suddenly had an excitement rush through me regarding our upcoming move to Chicago. I remember telling my friend, "Something has to be wrong with this picture...it doesn't make any sense!" I felt a total change of heart about our new orders to Chicago. I was excited and looking forward to it.

What was going on? I remember absolutely crediting God for this sudden change of attitude.

We had friends who were stationed at Great Lakes, Howard and Nikki. Bob contacted Howard and told him we would be moving to the area. Howard quickly told him "Quarters 63" was vacant and located across the street from where he lived. Howard was going to go talk to the Housing Personnel and see if there was any possibility of us being assigned to that particular house. Oh, by the way, he also informed us that the house had a reputation for being haunted! No big deal, who believes in that kind of stuff anyway?

After a few phone calls and some special arrangements, we were going to be assigned to "Quarters 63," as long as we could take possession by the end of January. Bob was not scheduled to rotate out of Camp Pendleton until March. However, exceptions were made, as long as I would move in by the end of January. We would vacate our quarters on base and Bob would move into the barracks at Camp Pendleton and I would move into Quarters 63 at Great Lakes.

Arrangements were quickly made for us to move out of our home at Camp Pendleton. Bob and I originally had planned on driving to Great Lakes and he was going to fly back, leaving me with a car. It sounded like a great plan, especially since I would be back there for a month before he could join me. As the weather remained inclement, we decided driving might not be the best idea after all, so we chose to fly instead. We were expecting to do a door-to-door move. (This means your household belongings would be packed up, loaded on the moving van and delivered directly to your new address within just a few days. This is an ideal situation since you would not have your things put in storage and then taken back out of storage to be delivered.) Bob would be there for a week to help me get settled before going back to Camp Pendleton. Well, that plan didn't work out very well, either. Due to the inclement weather, our moving truck was delayed. Instead of arriving early in the week, it didn't show up until Friday. Bob would be returning to California on Sunday.

We spent the week with our friends while we were waiting for our household goods to arrive. It was an interesting week, to say the least. Remember, our friend had casually mentioned that "our house" was haunted! Oh my goodness, all week long, we heard story after story about various incidents that had taken place in that house. I have never been one to give much thought to the possibility of "ghosts" and such, however, by the time I had heard multiple stories, it did make me think twice about it.

We even had a gentleman come to our door who was doing some research in the area, and they were actually putting plugs into the ground to test the soil and see if they could find any remnants of the mass graves that had been dug in the early 1900's. We were told there had been an epidemic of cholera that spread throughout the Navy base during that time. It is believed that one of the young Naval Academy graduates, McDuffy, fell victim to the rampant disease and died there. They believe he had either gone to school or lived in Quarters 63. Years later, when the school was converted into a single dwelling officer home, a sunporch room was added onto the side of it. Some believe McDuffy's body was probably buried beneath where the sunporch now existed and his spirit was disturbed. There were many other stories floating around telling of different tenants' experiences in the house with "McDuffy."

Even the lady from the housing office quickly told us, "This house comes with its own ghost — but not to worry, he is a friendly ghost and often plays tricks on you." She told us not to be surprised if the dishwasher comes on spontaneously or if we heard boxes being thrown down the stairs. She went on to tell some of her own stories. One story she shared had been told to her by a previous tenant. The tenant said that it was not uncommon for her to see a "ghostly-looking" enlisted man parading around the outside of the house in period uniform in the middle of the afternoon just as though he were patrolling the area on a "duty watch". We thought it was rather odd that she would be one to tell us anything at all about the ghost, McDuffy. Why would someone from housing want to tell us about that prior to moving in?

I will never forget our first night in the house. It was Friday night, and I had a dream. Now I know it was just a dream, but it was rather an unusual one. I remember being in a large room with lots of people. As I looked across the room I saw this ghostly figure of a man in a green plaid shirt and a top hat. He stood out from the rest of the crowd, not just by the clothes he was wearing, but also the fact that he was rather translucent, e.g., like one of the characters at Disney Land or Disney World in the haunted house — you know what I am talking about. Well, anyway, there he was and as I looked at him in my dream, I remember saying, "McDuffy, is that you?" He didn't say a word, but he bowed at the waist in acknowledgment of my question. I woke up, and that was the end of my dream. The next morning I told Bob I had met McDuffy during the night. I told him of my dream and we just laughed it off.

Saturday morning, our second day in the house, we received a UPS shipment. The first thing the carrier said to me when he delivered our package was "Quarters 63, the Haunted House! Did you know this house is listed in the Chicago Book of Haunts?" Oh, my goodness! I could hardly believe it! We soon checked it out and actually purchased the book because of the novelty of actually living in that house.

Sunday morning came and Bob flew back to Camp Pendleton. I was now on my own for a month in the big haunted house without a car. Now it is true, our friends did live across the street and were only a phone call away. Bob had made sure I was stocked up with plenty of food before he left. He knew I would have plenty to keep me busy over the next month, as I would be unpacking boxes and making our quarters, our new home.

At the end of the day, I had made many trips up and down the stairs trying to get everything in its right place. Each trip I made to the basement, I found myself thinking of all the "stories" I had just heard about this haunted house. Now I must say, if you were one that would be bothered by that, this was definitely not the place you would want to stay in by yourself.

One more thing about the basement: when you walked down to the bottom of the stairs, the laundry facility was right in front of you. There was a big board on the left wall that provided a crawl space for under the rest of the house. It was not a full basement. To the right of the stairs you would walk through an arched doorway into another room with a good sized open area and two more rooms. To the immediate left side of the open area were two restroom stalls. The toilets had been removed, but you could see where they had been located originally. Across from the stalls was the first room which looked like a bomb shelter—cement floor and walls with a steel door that could be padlocked. Across the open space to the right there was another room that we called the "jail" room. Also, in the "jail" room, at the far right side was another 3x3 crawl space with a sheet of plywood covering the opening. So you could enter one end of the crawl space in the laundry area and actually come out the other end in the jail room. There were lots of big and small pipes running across the ceiling of the basement area. It was definitely an interesting basement. Not one that you would necessarily feel comfortable going down into, especially if you were concerned about any of the ghost stories we had heard about.

Our bedroom was on the third floor. It was a

huge room, probably used as a classroom or possibly a barracks room with many beds. It was 14'x30'. There were two ceiling fans located at each end of the room. Our bed was centered under one of those fans. Now again, it was January and there was still snow on the ground, and there was definitely no need to have the fans running.

As I went to bed that night, I remember just whispering a prayer that God would give me *"peace"* and that I would not let all those stories I had heard bother me. Well, I have to tell you, in the middle of the night I suddenly woke up. It was as though fear itself had its arms wrapped around my stomach. I was literally paralyzed with fear. I couldn't speak, scream or cry out — not that any of that would have done any good. No one could have possibly heard me! The ceiling fan was on and I had not turned it on! As the moments passed, and I was unable to speak, suddenly only one word came out of my mouth. I cried out "JESUS!" That is all I could say. But as soon as I said the name of Jesus, I watched that fan slow down and come to a complete stop! The most incredible *"peace"* filled that room and my spirit. I was able to lay my head down on my pillow and go right back to sleep.

I found myself the next couple of days thinking about that experience, wondering what it was all about. Was there really a ghost in the house named McDuffy? Did he turn the ceiling fan on? I was asking God about this and I sensed Him speaking to my heart, "It wasn't a ghost, but it was spiritual warfare!" (Ephesians 6:12 "For our struggle is not against flesh and blood, but against the rulers, against the authorities, against the powers of this dark world and against the spiritual forces of evil in the heavenly realms". (NIV))

I believe God planned from the beginning for us to go to Great Lakes. He had changed my attitude to the point I was looking forward to our tour there. I believed He would open up ministry opportunities for me to be involved in. I also believe, Satan, the Devil or whatever you choose to call him, also had his work cut out for him. You see, he will do whatever it takes to get us off track from God's purposes. He had a perfect opportunity to thwart my enthusiasm and my ministry effectiveness. After all, we were moving into a house that is actually documented in the Chicago Book of Haunts for its "ghostly" happenings. He made sure I heard all kinds of stories, right from the start, about supernatural happenings in that house. It was a perfect opportunity to instill fear into my heart.

Fear can be paralyzing in more ways than one. If I was full of fear, I would've hated living in that house. If I'd hated living in that house, I would probably not have been focused on what God wanted me to do for Him. I would be dreading each night spent there and looking forward to our tour passing as quickly as possible.

As it turned out, I never again felt the spirit of fear in that house after that memorable night. I actually believe that experience triggered a huge victory for Jesus, and the enemy was defeated. I thoroughly enjoyed living in that home for the nearly two years we were there. Going into the basement became exciting for me. It was pretty interesting, and I loved the opportunity to live in that historic home. The ghost stories just added to the experience.

Some have asked if we had any other experiences during our time there. As a matter of fact, we did have a couple more instances. But there was no fear attached to either of them. Three times, the shower would come on all by itself. Once was in the middle of the night! The other two times, it came on after we left the house. But it really didn't matter. I had the *"peace"* only God can provide while we lived there.

The experiences I had at Great Lakes were a true highlight in our military career. I loved that old house with all its mystery.

It turned out to be a season of great ministry. I hosted a small group ladies' Bible Study in our home. Later, I found myself working at a Thomas Kinkade Art Gallery where I had tremendous ministry opportunities on a daily basis.

The reason I share this story with you is to remind you of the tremendous *"power"* in the name of Jesus. I found supernatural *"peace"* when I cried out the name of "Jesus!" in that moment of paralyzing fear. I don't care what kind of fear or circumstances you may be facing, Jesus is waiting for us to call on his name. He wants to bless us with his *"peace"* and meet us where we are so we can fulfill his *"purpose"* in our lives. Don't let fear ever keep you from the joy you will find in doing the things God has created for you to do.

"And the peace of God, which transcends all understanding will guard your hearts and your minds in Christ Jesus."
Philippians 4:7 (NIV)

Discover Peace in the Midst of Your Trials

I want to share one final story and the last "P" for *"Peace"* with you as we conclude this study. God not only provides a way through Jesus Christ for us to know Him on a personal level, but He is also eager to walk through life with us as His children, and give us all the *Power, Purpose, Possibilities* and *"Peace"* we need to face whatever challenge life brings our way.

My late husband, Bob, went home to be with Jesus on January 27, 2014. I want to briefly tell you of God's amazing *"Peace"* through my journey with him.

I mentioned earlier, my husband had been in the U.S. Navy for seven years as an enlisted sailor, then felt God's calling on him to become a chaplain. This meant he would break from the Navy to attend seminary, and then return for an additional 29 years as a chaplain and an officer. At this point in time, he had been a chaplain for 25 years and had just been promoted to Chief of Chaplains of the entire U.S. Navy.

He had gone in for his annual physical when his cancer was discovered. Looking at him, he was a picture of health! When we received this diagnosis, he was in Stage II of Multiple Myeloma, and it had already impacted 65% of his bone marrow without a single symptom. It was the most surreal moment of my life! This news did not hit me with the emotion of tears, I just remember feeling numb to it all.

After we called our family, I laid in bed that night unable to go to sleep. I was laying there playing out the worst case scenarios in my mind. I suddenly had this most amazing conversation with God, not audible, but very clearly spoken to my heart. I was feeling overwhelmed and the tears were beginning to flow when God began speaking to me, "Evelyn, what are you trying to do? You are trying to figure out the end of my plan, and that is not for you to know. This cancer is not about you or Bob, it is about my Glory! Your job is to trust me! This is going to be a test of your faith." When He said the word "test" my response was "I don't do well at tests, Lord."

He quickly reminded me of the Israelites in the Old Testament when He supplied manna for them. They were instructed not to gather it up for more than one day at a time except before the Sabbath, or it would go bad on them. He said, "This is how my peace, grace and strength are going to be supplied to you, one day at a time." He went on to say, "I have entrusted you with this journey." Now when someone entrusts you with something, it totally changes the perspective! God didn't put this journey on us, but he entrusted it to us. There is a big difference.

That night I remember telling God I knew Bob had been a gift to me from Him and I knew first of all, he belonged to God. I recall telling Him, if He would receive more glory by taking Bob home to be with Him, I would accept that. However, my prayer would continue to be for healing for my husband. I asked Him to forgive me for allowing my mind to race to all the negative "what if's?". I also promised that when the natural negative thoughts would begin to come and want to sink into my heart and mind, I would not dwell on them, but would use them as a reminder to thank God for the grace and the strength He promised to give me for this journey. This was a test of faith I wanted to pass to honor God.

My husband went through a very successful stem cell transplant and it took the cancer down to less than one percent in his body. We were excited! I truly believed that we had passed our test of faith triumphantly. Bob was in a place of high leadership and visibility, and people were watching our lives to see how we handled this test.

It is one thing to live out your faith when things are going great and life is good. But what does your faith look like when things don't go the way you want them to go? For nearly five years, cancer wasn't even on our minds. The doctors tried to warn us the cancer would come back; it could not be completely cured, but I had believed it was a once in a lifetime experience. The cancer was pretty much gone and we had passed our test with flying colors.

A year after he retired, the cancer came again like a shock wave, and he went through a second stem-cell transplant. This time it was not as successful and only bought him nine more months before the cancer returned and began to spread out of control for a third time.

Toward the end, there was a time during one of his hospital stays when we received PET scan results and the reality of the invasion of this cancer hit home to me. I remember feeling like I couldn't handle any more. I thought I was going to collapse as I was reading the words "innumerable spots of cancer throughout his entire body."

At that very point, God showed me in my mind's eye that I was standing at a "T" in the road. One sign pointed to the right and read "My Peace and My Strength". The other sign pointed to the left and read "Your Emotions, Tears, Headache, Swollen Eyes and Despair". I needed to decide which way I was going to go. My head and heart knew the only right way to go was with the Lord's *"Peace"* and Strength. He was reminding me that He was still there to continue to supply all I needed. Everything within me cried out to go with my emotions. At that moment I cried out to God and asked for His help, and He said, "Let's go, I will carry you!"

I believe there is a "slippery slope of sorrow" that is the natural progression for people to slip into when they lose someone or something precious in their life. I truly believe God has literally carried me right over the top of the deep pit of sorrow. It doesn't mean I haven't had my moments, but that is what it has amounted to, "brief moments". Then, God has reminded me that "I can do all things with

His help and strength." My spirit is encouraged, and I have been able to move forward. He has given me the *"peace"* that truly passes all understanding. I have learned He is trustworthy and true to His promises!

My husband and I were married over 45 years! He battled cancer off and on for about seven years, and then he received his eternal set of orders! Destination: Heaven. As my son-in-law, Jeremy Johnson said so well at his Celebration of Life service, "Although we will miss him, Dad was never one to turn down orders!"

- Read Philippians 4:6-7.

- Don't worry about anything? Make a list of the things you worry about. Leave room next to each worry.

- Take a look at each concern above. Pray that God would replace your worry with peace. Next to each worry, write "Thank You for Your Peace" and trust that God is with you in your circumstance.

- Sometimes, it helps to get the arrows off ourselves when we are struggling to think of others. Do you have a friend who is going through something difficult right now? Write them a letter or an email or send them a text with this scripture, letting them know they are not alone and that you are praying for peace in their heart.

1. What about a spiritual or emotional storm? How was God with you?

2. What was the biggest worry you wrote down in your personal reflection time? Has God given you peace about it?

3. Where do you need God's peace right now?

4. What is something this group can pray with you about as we end this study?

"For God so loved the world that He gave his one and only Son, that whoever believes in him shall not perish but have eternal life."

John 3:16 (NIV)

Personal Challenge of Faith!

If you sense God prompting you, and you know in your heart this personal relationship with God is lacking in your life, I encourage you by faith to invite Jesus into your life. Let him wash away all your sins and past failures and remove the guilt from your life. He is in the business of trading in our old lives and giving us brand new ones. We may look the same on the outside, but he does a heart transplant spiritually on the inside. It is the single most important decision any of us will ever make. It is the first step we must take to allow our lives to take on new meaning and purpose.

If you have never invited Jesus to come into your life, I want to encourage you to do that now. My prayer is that these stories have touched your heart. God loves you more than anyone else is capable of loving you. He created you and He has a planned Destiny for your life.

As I have pointed out through several of my stories, God has made arrangements for our sins to be forgiven and forgotten through His only son, Jesus. Jesus took the guilt and shame of all we have ever done and paid the penalty for our sins when he died on the cross. All we have to do is accept grace and surrender our life to him. "If we confess our sins, he is faithful and just and will forgive us our sins and purify us from all unrighteousness." 1 John 1:9 (NIV)

The best part of "His" story is, Jesus didn't just die with our sins, but rose again on the third day and is now living in heaven with God. He is preparing a home for us where we can live forever with him and experience no more sorrow or pain! He has sent the Holy Spirit to be with us on earth, to comfort, guide and teach us the right way to live. "Do not let your hearts be troubled. Trust in God; trust also in me. In my Father's house are many rooms; if it were not so, I would have told you, I will come back and take you to be with me that you also may be where I am. You know the way to the place where I am going." John 14:1-4 (NIV)

You can live as a Person of Destiny—all four P's are yours for the taking!

"Therefore, if anyone is in
Christ, the new creation has
come: the old is gone, the
new is here!"
2 Corinthians 5:17 (NIV)

Prayer for New Life

If you are ready to begin a new life, living as a Person of Destiny in Jesus, I invite you to pray this prayer now:

"Dear Jesus, I want to know you and experience the love you have for me. I invite you to come into my life and forgive me for all my sins. Thank you for paying the penalty for my sins when you died on the cross. I ask you to give me a brand new start in my life with you. Please help me to live out the Destiny you had in mind when you created me. I ask you to fill me with your *purpose, power, possibilities* and *peace.* Help me to honor you by living my life for you. I love you and thank you. In Jesus' Name, I pray. Amen."

If you have prayed this prayer for the first time, **"Welcome to the family of God!"** The Bible tells us, "Therefore, if anyone is in Christ, he is a new creation; the old has gone, the new has come!" And He died for all, that those who live should no longer live for themselves but for him who died for them and was raised again." 2 Corinthians 5:17-19 (NIV)

"Do your best to present yourself to God as one approved, a worker who does not need to be ashamed and who correctly handles the word of truth."
2 Timothy 2:15 (NIV)

Helpful Hints for Living With Destiny

1. Talk to God each day and thank Him for His love for you and the many ways He has blessed your life. Offer worship and praise to Him because He is so worthy of it. He has forgiven you of your sins, and He has a Destiny in mind for your life. Ask Him to be with you and to help you to walk in His ways and be mindful of Him. Use this conversation time to share your concerns.

2. Read your Bible every day. There are many great devotionals to help you get started. Reading one chapter of Proverbs each day is a great way to gain knowledge and insight into God's word. Ask God to speak to you through the verses you read.

3. Memorize scripture. It will help you keep your mind focused on God and help keep you from sinning. When you are reading your Bible, if a particular verse stands out to you, underline it and put it to memory!

4. Find a good church to attend that teaches the Bible, God's Word.

5. Join a Small Group and grow together in the Lord with other believers. Our church has a saying: "No one does the mission alone".

6. Ask God for Christian friends that will

encourage you in your new life. Find a mentor who will walk with you in your new journey.

7. Share with others what God is doing in your life.

8. Become a mentor to someone and help them grow.

Reading Challenge

"If you want to find real transformation in your life as a Christian, try reading the four Gospels, Matthew, Mark, Luke and John, four times each in thirty days."

I heard this challenge presented many years ago. At the time, it seemed impossible! I did not even realize I had logged it into my memory bank.

However, it came back to me recently, as I was encouraging a new Christian to read the Gospel of Mark to help her get to know Jesus a little better. I had suggested reading the book of Mark since it was the shortest of the four Gospels and action packed. I told her if she had any questions, don't hesitate to call me. I wasn't trying to say I had all the answers but that I was pretty familiar with it, and if I didn't have an answer, I would find one.

I decided maybe it would be a good idea for me to read it again, to refresh myself in case she did have questions. So I started reading it from start to finish. I had barely started reading when suddenly the challenge I had heard so many years before popped into my head. For some reason, the timing was right, and I decided to take the challenge on. What I discovered was life changing. I have read through the Bible many times over the years, but there is something that takes place when you read one book four times each before moving on to the next one. I never once found it to be boring, but quite the opposite! It piqued my interest in reading the Bible.

You know, repetition is one of our best ways to learn. Since then, I decided to read through the entire New Testament that way. It was great! I would read the book in a different translation each time. It seemed to open up my heart and mind to understand it even better with each reading. I became passionate about reading God's word, and found it to really transform my way of thinking about reading the scriptures.

I hope you will consider taking on this Bible reading challenge. I believe it can be a powerful step in your growing relationship with God.

ADDITIONAL READING SUGGESTIONS

- Purpose Driven Life, by Rick Warren

- A Woman after God's Own Heart, by Elizabeth George

- Circle Maker, by Mark Batterson

"If I speak with the tongues of men or of angels, but have not love, I am only a resounding gong or a clanging symbol."

1 Corinthians 13:1 (NIV)

Initiating Conversations to Share Christ

In our fresh enthusiasm for God and a desire to share this great news with others, there are some things we need to keep in mind. Not everyone is going to be as enthusiastic to hear your good news as you are to share it. That being said, I can assure you there will be plenty of opportunities for you to speak boldly and with confidence to those God is preparing to hear what you have to say. The verse on the previous page is a powerful reminder that when we speak to others, we must speak with sincere love and concern for them if we expect to be heard. Just spilling out a bunch of knowledge of God without love and compassion for the one we are speaking to has the power to turn them off toward hearing the Gospel message. That is not the kind of sharing we want to be be a part of.

We must remember, that there are a lot of factors to consider. Think about how you came to know Jesus. Did you accept him the first time you heard about him? Probably not! Some people may have had a bad church experience or even a bad relationship with someone who they perceived to be a Christian. This experience may cause them to be skeptical or not open to hearing what you have to say. We must respect other people and be sensitive to the right opportunity or timing to speak to them. This is where the power of the Holy Spirit comes in.

I would like to share some personal prerequisites that I have found to be very helpful to me. These are in no way hard, fast rules, only suggestions for you to consider:

1. Make sure you are in the "Word" (the Bible) on a regular basis.

2. Be consistently growing in your personal relationship with God through prayer and Bible Study.

These first two steps set you up to be more sensitive to hearing God speaking to you. You are learning to recognize His voice through the printed word in the Bible, which is the predominate way He speaks to us. Praying or having conversation with Him and taking time to sit quietly and allow the Holy Spirit to speak to your heart is a powerful discipline in developing your ability to hear and recognize His voice when He speaks to your Spirit.

3. Pray specifically for God to use your testimony of what He has done in your life to be a blessing and/or encouragement to others.

4. Be prepared and intentional about looking for an opportunity to speak to someone.

5. Ask God to provide someone ready to hear and/or receive.

I often will look for opportunity to engage in a conversation with someone. It can be anywhere. Sometimes waiting rooms provide great opportunity to meet new people, i.e. hospitals, doctor's offices, military pharmacies, particularly when you know there is going to be a period of time just sitting around and waiting.

As I shared in an earlier story, I have found sometimes sitting next to someone on an airplane has provided me with many opportunities to engage in worthwhile conversation that allows me to share my story of faith. Again, you must be sensitive to their receptivity. If I am sitting by someone who has their headset on or is totally engaged in reading a book, I will typically not try to interrupt them. However, I have found many people will welcome conversation as a way of making time go by more quickly.

I will start out with something very generic. On a plane, I will start out by introducing myself to them. I may ask them where they are headed. Is it business or pleasure? I listen for something I can identify with. Maybe I have visited the place they are going, and I may mention something about it. I am not trying to pry into their personal business, just expressing interest. Most people are fine with sharing that kind of information. In turn, I will tell them where I am going and maybe even what is taking me there! It's at that point, I will usually tell a little about myself, and most generally incorporate God into that information. I have many personal stories to draw from that speak of God's provision, comfort, or strength in a situation.

After sharing briefly a little personal story about myself, I may ask them, "How about you? Do you have any faith background?" Their response to that question will usually provide me with enough information to know whether they are interested in hearing anything more about God and faith. I listen to what they have to say. If I sense they really don't understand a personal relationship with Jesus, but have appeared to be receptive to what I have said so far, I will take the conversation a little deeper. I try not to be judgmental about any part of their story, but rather carefully and prayerfully ask God to give me guidance.

I believe this type of interaction gives me opportunity to plant a thought that may direct them to give more careful consideration to what God may want to do in their life. I want to share something that will cause them to consider and even ponder again and again, long after our conversation. I once heard it said that it takes the average person more than six times of hearing the Gospel story before they are ready to make a decision for Christ. I want to be one of those six times they hear the message. You never know when you will be the sixth person and they are ready to receive Christ into their own life.

Try to have some scriptures memorized that will point them to their need for Christ and the provision God has made for them.

There is group of scriptures referred to as the "Romans Road" that can help lead you through the verses that point to our need for Christ in our life. I encourage you to take a moment to Google "Romans Road" for a complete listing of the scriptures and familiarize yourself with them and even memorize them. But at the very least, have a list of them handy on your notepad, on your phone, or in something else that you can easily carry with you. That way, when the opportunity presents itself, you will be equipped and prepared.

I usually carry a small New Testament with me to share these verses if the opportunity allows. I don't do it every time I talk to someone, but only when I feel the Holy Spirit nudging me to do so. I will invite the person to read the scripture out loud for him or herself, if they will, and then ask them what the scripture says to them. It is amazing to me that every time I have ever done that, the person has understood clearly what the scripture is saying. The cool part is I am not pushing on them my own interpretation of scripture, but giving them the opportunity to see it from their own understanding. I believe this has a powerful effect.

The opportunity to pray with someone when they are truly ready to invite Christ into their life is truly an emotional high for me. It certainly doesn't happen every time, however, it does happen! God doesn't ask me to "save" people. Only He has the power to do that. But He does expect me to share His love with others in such a way that they are able to hear about Him.

After I have had the opportunity to speak to someone, I will usually conclude the conversation, by letting them know I will be praying for them as often as God brings them to mind.

It never ceases to amaze me the many times God will remind me to pray for that person. I may never see them again on the face of this earth, but I am thankful for the opportunity I was given to speak truth, hope, and faith into their lives with genuine love and concern. Just like I am thankful for the opportunity I have been given to speak truth, hope, and faith into your life as you have read this book.

May God bless you!